D0277717

CONTENTS

PHOTO CREDITS: Covers and front endpapers by Harry V. Lacey. Back endpapers by Dr. Matthew Vriends. These photographs show the various color varieties of the society, or Bengalese, finch. The title page photograph shows three chicks from the same nest. Bred and photographed by the author.

Color photos: Mervin F. Roberts, Harry V. Lacey, Horst Mueller, Louise Van der Meid. Black and white photos: Mervin F. Roberts, Harry V. Lacey, Dr. Herbert R. Axelrod.

ISBN 0-87666-990-9

KW-029

© 1979 by T.F.H. Publications, Inc. LTD.

Distributed in the U.S. by T.F.H. Publications, Inc., 211 West Sylvania Avenue, P.O. Box 427, Neptune, N.J. 07753; in England by T.F.H. (Gt. Britain) Ltd., 13 Nutley Lane, Reigate, Surrey; in Canada to the book store and library trade by Beaverbooks, 953 Dillingham Road, Picker-ing, Ontario L1W 1Z7; in Canada to the pet trade by Rolf C. Hagen Ltd., 3225 Sartelon Street, Montreal 382, Quebec; in Southeast Asia by Y.W. Ong, 9 Lorong 36 Geylang, Singapore 14; in Australia and the South Pacific by Pet Imports Pty. Ltd., P.O. Box 149, Brookvale 2100, N.S.W., Australia; in South Africa by Valiant Publishers (Pty.) Ltd., P.O. Box 78236, Sandton City, 2146, South Africa; Published by T.F.H. Publica-tions, Inc., Ltd., The British Crown Colony of Hong Kong.

SOCIETY FINCHES

by MERVIN F. ROBERTS

Silverbill finches also have muted colors following the same basic hues as the society finch. There are two species of silverbills. One is from Africa (the bird on the right) and one from India.

Society, or Bengalese, finches are very popular and exist only as domesticated birds, much like the dog breeds. There are three basic color varieties: pure white, cinnamon and white and chocolate brown and white. Because of their mixed background no two birds are marked exactly the same.

Youngsters just leaving the nest. If they were hand-fed they would make excellent pets. The photo below shows the typical pet shop scene with hundreds of finches kept together.

Introduction

When this author was a boy a formal introduction was required before any really serious conversation could commence. Names and addresses were taken seriously, remembered and recorded with fidelity. Now, at least in the U.S. of A., the custom has changed dramatically. Parents of eligible daughters consider themselves lucky if they can discover their intended son-in-law's full and correct name in time to print the wedding invitations. This carelessness with names carries over to our pets as well. Tens of thou-

Society finches are found in several forms. No two individual birds are colored alike. Solid colors, such as the chocolate (topmost) and cinnamon (bottommost) are called "selfs."

Bronze-winged mannikin, *Lonchura cucullata.*

Common spice finch, sometimes referred to as the nutmeg mannikin, *Lonchura punctulata.*

sands of one species of cage bird known for perhaps 250 years in the British Isles as *"Bengalese"* finches are bought, bred, exhibited and sold in the United States as *"society"* finches. It has also sometimes been called a *"munia."* It has also sometimes been called a *"mannikin."* Same bird. Same language. This makes a formal introduction awkward. And that's the way the cookie crumbles.

It is most probable that the names "society," "munia," and "mannikin" will eventually be dropped in favor of "Bengalese" because most of the scientific literature, exhibiting, establishment of standards, and controlled breeding is being carried out by people who call these birds "Bengalese." The National Bengalese Fanciers Association (NBFA) is in fact *the* international organization. There are NBFA affiliated clubs and individual members all over the world, and their name will surely prevail.

There is a good deal of hobbyist literature about Bengalese finches in Europe, but in the Americas only recently has there been much interest in this bird on the part of the general pet-keeping public. Since this book was written by an American and manufactured in the U.S.A., it will reflect current custom here, and so between these covers this species will be mostly referred to as the society finch or even more simply as the society. All else about it remains the same, worldwide.

There isn't very much you *must* know about society finches in order to enjoy them. They are hardy and long-lived. Their requirements are simple. The paraphernalia you need to buy is inexpensive. Your pet shop dealer probably told you enough in a few minutes so that you could carry your birds through the next few years. Why then this book and its companion volume, *Breeding Society Finches*? Let's begin by considering what we have.

The society finch is neither noisy nor musical, but it does have a cheery chirp. This appeals to many bird keepers who are fed up with whistles, squeaks, raucous squawks and mimicry. Society finch colors are muted; they are never yellow, red, green or blue. Their colors range from either chocolate (or cinnamon) paling to white, and their plumage is usually trim and sleek. The fanciest variation in feathering to date is a modest crest, or rosette, of feathers crowning the head to create the impression of a perpetual frown.

Your society finch will perform no funny antics. It is not an acrobat or a clown, as are many of the parrot-like birds. If there was ever a low-key aviary bird, this is it. But you bought it. Many other people also have bought them. Among the small cage birds it is one of the top five in popularity. *Something* about the society finch appeals to people. Look at its name, "society finch." Socially, this bird gets along well with other birds and also with people. It has been a domesticated bird for centuries. As to the finch part of its name, it is not, technically speaking, a true finch—more about that later.

Although its appeal is hard to define, it is a well established cage bird in many parts of the world. Fanciers buy them, breed them, exhibit them, judge them and study their genetics as intently as do breeders of racehorses. Although there may be no rational explanation of their popularity, the fact remains: society finches are popular cage and aviary pets. As we look closely, many of us are drawn even more closely. Simply stated they appeal to people.

Basic care is easy, but with very little additional effort you can give your pets assurance of long and healthy lives. With additional knowledge about what makes them tick, you can enjoy them more as you get to know them better. That is what this book is all about.

If you have a pair, they will probably want to raise a family, and this won't be too difficult for them or for you. What you read here will help you get started with a breeding pair, but if you should become more involved in propagating these birds, you might want to read the companion text entitled *Breeding Society Finches*.

13

Shafttail finch from Australia.

Cherry finch, *Poephila acuticauda acuticauda*.

1. Pintailed nonpareil. 2. Masked grassfinch. 3. Chestnut-breasted finch. 4. Star finch.

This zebra finch is a really mixed-up bird. One side has the coloration of a male, while the other side has the coloration of a female. The view below shows the male side while the head-on view shows how it is split. Photos by Lacey.

Classification

As just mentioned, your society finches are not true finches. And it is unlikely that the parent stock was native to Bengal. Ornithologists generally agree that the true finches are in the family Fringillidae, the family that includes bullfinches, chaffinches, canaries, hawfinches, sparrows, greenfinches, grosbeaks, crossbills, linnets, siskins, goldfinches, redpolls, bobolinks and buntings. Those birds are primarily natives of the temperate regions of the northern hemisphere. The society finches *had* at one time been placed by classifiers in the family Ploceidae, where we find the weavers and still other mostly tropical African, Australian and Asiatic forms.

Kingdom: ANIMALIA: Animal.

Phylum: CHORDATA: Chordates, with a central nervous system dorsally situated. This excludes single-celled animals, mollusks, insects, worms, etc.

Subphylum: VERTEBRATA: Vertebrates, with cartilage or bony spinal column enclosing at least part of the central nervous system.

Class: AVES: Birds. Warm-blooded, feathered, egg-laying vertebrates. 9000 species, 28 orders.

Order: PASSERIFORMES: Birds that perch and sing. They have four toes on each foot. The toes are joined at the same level; three always point forward. (By contrast, the owls and parrots have two toes forward and two aft on each foot.) There are no webs between the toes. Young are nidicolous; that is, they are hatched naked, blind, helpless. Generally parents take good care of their young, but a few species are nest parasites. There are more than 60 families, containing 5100 species.

Family: ESTRILDIDAE: commonly called estrildid weavers. Here, according to some authorities, we have the waxbills, grassfinches and mannikins. Nestlings have decorated palates and tongues. Nestlings beg for food by crouching with mouths opened wide, waving their heads. Estrildids mature rapidly, often in only a few months. There are 125 species, including zebra finches and Java sparrows.

OR

Family: PLOCEIDAE. 136 species including weavers, widowbirds and sparrows. (Over the course of years, orni-

18

thologists have re-evaluated and re-classified many families of birds. This book is not the place to solve these problems).

Genus: *LONCHURA:* The name of the genus means "lance bearer," because of the birds' long pointed tail feathers.

Species: *DOMESTICA:* The domesticated one.

If we follow this particular route we end up with the society or Bengalese finch neatly and scientifically boxed in as *Lonchura domestica.*

BUT between 1963 and the time of this writing, we have all these following names from recognized authorities in this field:

Lonchura domestica (Bates and Busenbark, 1963)
Lonchura striata dom. (R.L. Restall, 1975)
Lonchura striata domestica (J. Buchan, 1975)
Lonchura domestica (M. Vriends, 1976)
Uroloncha domestica (V. Clear, 1966)
Munia domestica (K.J. Lawrence circa 1973).

Don't be upset or annoyed if you discover in another book that there are not 9000 but actually only 8600 species of birds or that there are not 28 but only 27 orders of birds. Even if you are anti-hunting, don't blame it all on hunters and, if you are anti-insecticide, don't blame it all on the chemicals. The four hundred species or the missing order did not become extinct through hunting or poisoning. Rather, credit the loss to ornithological classifiers who, between books, lumped some species and reclassified certain populations as subspecies rather than species. Same thing obtains for a lost order or two.

This book is about a bird which makes a good case in point. At one time the genesis of the domestic society finch was unknown, and some ornithologists granted it status as a species. Later, Erica Eisner concluded after study of the evidence that it is really a selectively bred subspecies of a common wild bird. Things like that happen all the time in the classification of living things. The end is not in sight.

Erica Eisner of Oxford, England, in *Aviculture Magazine* 1957, pages 101 through 108, attempted to clarify the status of our society finch, but many authors subsequently ignored her work. What she had to say bears repeating. She begins with A. G. Butler, who in 1894 wrote a book entitled *Foreign Finches in Captivity* (L. Reeve & Co., London). In this book Butler suggested a hybrid origin for what he called the Bengalese and we call the society finch. The book was popular and is still considered worthwhile reading. In 1907 Butler reversed himself, but that reversal was not in a popular book, and so it was largely ignored.

Erica Eisner goes on to point out that striated and sharp-tailed finches are both members of the same species, *Lonchura striata*. These two subspecies are easy to recognize and separate.

Striated finches are found in Ceylon and India. In this subspecies the brown parts are very dark, nearly black on the head and breast, while the rump and the belly are almost white. The tail feathers are not pointed, as are those of the sharp-tailed.

Sharp-tailed finches are native to the lands from Nepal and Bengal to Malaya and China. The sharp-tailed does have that sharp pointing of the long tail feathers; furthermore, its dark parts do not tend to black but rather to a less deep, more reddish brown.

Eisner compared the domesticated Bengalese with both wild subspecies and concluded that it has all the characteristics of the sharp-tailed and none of the striated or of any other wild bird. She also notes that Dr. Desmond Morris compared the behavior of the domestic bird with that of other species and found that the society resembled in action only the sharp-tailed.

E.C. Stuart Baker, in 1926 wrote *The Fauna of British India: Birds*, Vol. III, Second Edition, Taylor and Francis, London, and in it the recognized three color varieties, which he ranked as subspecies:

Lonchura striata acuticauda—Nepal and Bengal

L. s. subsquamicollis—Burma, Indo-China, Malaya and Sumatra

L. s. squamicollis—China.

Erica Eisner points out the inadequacy of Stuart Baker's descriptions and analysis in that it does not suggest a trend of change in color across China, which the British Museum skins seem to establish. She also points out that the authoritative Japanese Taka-Tsukasa told us in 1922 that the Japanese stock came from China about 200 years ago.

Further comparison of skins in the British Museum with live birds leads her to the conclusion that the ancestral stock of our bird is to be found in Fukien, China or Taiwan.

If you become interested in breeding society finches, you will also want to know the names of those species which have been hybridized with our *L. domestica*.

Striated Munia (*Lonchura striata*), fertile offspring. This reinforces E. Eisner's opinion that the society is simply a domesticated *L. striata*.

White-rumped Mannikin, Sharp-tailed finch, a subspecies of the above mentioned *L. striata* (*Lonchura striata acuticauda*), fertile offspring when mated back to societies.

Chestnut-breasted Finch (*Lonchura castaneothorax*)

Black-beaked Bronze Mannikin (*Lonchura leucogastroides*)

Two-colored Mannikin (*Lonchura bicolor*)

Common Spice Finch, Nutmeg Mannikin (*Lonchura punctulata*)

Bronze-winged Mannikin (*Lonchura [Spermestes] cucullatus, Lonchura cucullata*)

1

2

3

Dusky Mannikin (*Lonchura fuscans*)

Rufous-backed Mannikin (*Spermestes bicolor nigriceps, Lonchura nigriceps*)

Magpie Mannikin (*Lonchura fringilloides*)

Pale-headed Mannikin (*Lonchura maja*)

African Silverbill (*Lonchura [Euodice] malabarica cantans)*

Indian Silverbill (*Lonchura malabarica malabarica*)

Chestnut Mannikin (*Lonchura malacca*)

Black-headed Mannikin, Chocolate Mannikin (*Lonchura malacca atricapilla*)

Dwarf Mannikin, Bib Finch (*Lonchura nana, Lemuresthes nana*)

Java Sparrow (*Padda oryzivora*)

Zebra Finch (*Poephila [Taeniopygia] guttata castanotis*)

Long-tailed Grassfinch (*Poephila acuticauda*)

Parson Finch (*Poephila cincta*)

Cherry Finch (*Poephila modesta*)

Masked Grassfinch (*Poephila personata*)

Bicheno Finch (*Poephila [Stizoptera] bichenovii*)

Star Finch (*Poephila [Bathilda] ruficauda*)

Cordon Bleu (*Granatina bengalus, Estrilda bengala*)

Cut-throat (*Amadina fasciata*)

Red-throated Parrot-Finch (*Erythrura psittacea*)

Diamond Sparrow (*Stagonopleura guttata, Zonaeginthus guttatus*)

If you wish to carry this any further, the best route is *via* Annie P. Gray in *Bird Hybrids*, Commonwealth Agricultural Bureaux, Farnham Royal, Bucks, England, 1958. Her list and its references for this species occupy about six pages of fine print.

1. Bicheno finch, 2. Two shafttail finches. 3. Strawberry finches.

Three colored society finches, two cinnamon and white and one chocolate and white. The natural perches of various thicknesses are ideal for society finches. The photo below shows all the color varieties, from pure white to selfs and pieds. These photos show the author's birds in the author's aviaries.

Varieties

The variety of names offers no problem. Call it domesticated munia or Bengalese or society, it is the same bird. When you compare a society finch with a pigeon, a budgerigar or a chicken, it doesn't offer much variety in the way of color or feather arrangement. The color ranges are between chocolate and white and also between cinnamon and white. That's about all! A modest crest is also available.

Let's start with the basic bird and then consider the variations. Look at a sharp-tailed mannikin. This "wild" munia is probably the progenitor or certainly one of the progenitors of the domesticated society. It has no pure white feathers and no jet black feathers. It has a dark upper bill and dark feet. The darkest feather in its plumage is a dark chocolate, the lightest is a very pale mocha. Call it a "self"

colored bird. In other species of domesticated birds a "self" is one solid color all over. Here we call a specimen which has few or no white feathers a "self." (Now that you have familiarized yourself with "self" it will no longer be placed within quotation marks.)

"Pied" is another word used frequently by bird keepers. Technically, one white feather makes a pied, but practically speaking a chocolate self is a rare bird and when you are getting started, you may be willing to settle for a self with a few white feathers.

"Dilute" is the third color term you will have to cope with as you discuss, describe, exhibit, buy, sell, trade and perhaps breed these little fellows. This is a washed-out chocolate or cinnamon. It blends all the way to white and is invariably pied with white.

"Fawn," also called "cinnamon," is another established term in the color lexicon you will need to know. The words are sufficiently expressive. Fawn birds may be self or pied with white or dilute which blends to white and is pied with white. All fawns and dilute fawns have ruby eyes—but eye color is very difficult to recognize, even with the bird-in-hand. Fawn birds have pale bills and pink feet.

White is white, almost. The variable here comes from the ancestry of a white bird. It may have been developed from a fawn or may have come from a strain of chocolates. The whites derived from chocolate strains have brown eyes, and the whites derived from fawn strains have ruby eyes. At least one strain of whites derived from fawns is prone to blindness. Perhaps all are. Neither of these aforementioned whites are albinos. At this time (1979) there are no pink-eyed society finches. Past experience with other domestic animals suggests that some day a strain of albinos will be established. This is a matter of chance mutation and not a matter of tedious selective breeding. An albino is just as likely to be hatched in a nest of self-chocolates as in a nest of fawn-derived whites.

Breeders do come up with tri-colors (chocolate-fawn-white) from time to time, but these birds are not established as varieties because the trait is not transmitted to their offspring. New subtle color variations do crop up and are given names by breeders. Eventually some will be accepted by hobbyists and others will be forgotten.

By way of review, your society finch is colored:

Self chocolate

Pied chocolate

Dilute chocolate and white

White with brown eyes

Self fawn

Pied fawn

Dilute fawn and white

White with ruby eyes

Seven categories if we combine the two whites and eight if we make note of the eyes on the whites.

Plumage is the other variable. Your healthy adult society finches will be sleek. There are usually no ruffles or flourishes on this bird. A crested or rosetted mutation does exist, but its genetic status is still not clear. We do know that crested birds usually produce crested offspring, but they do not necessarily breed 100% true.

There are some breeders who find that their best crested birds are derived from one crested parent and one non-crested. Other breeders have reported that this is not so and that excellent results come from a mating of two crested birds. It may be that "crested" is actually several mutations and these genetic traits are carried on several chromosomes—or in several positions on one chromosome.

In a cage or aviary the choice of color or plumage of the birds is up to you. They all get along perfectly well with each other. They all live a long time and, with the one possible caution about blindness in whites of fawn derivation, you should have no trouble caring for any of these varieties.

A typical nest of six eggs. Below, a bird market in Moscow (1978) where finches and other birds are traded between bird lovers. The world is slowly accepting the standards set by the National Bengalese Fanciers Association.

The National Bengalese Fanciers Association

This chapter and the "Exhibiting" chapter were written by Mr. E. J. (Ted) Hounslow of Gwent, South Wales and Mr. Norman Tolmaer of Sussex, England. These gentlemen are among the founders of the National Bengalese Fanciers Association (N.B.F.A.); at the time of this writing Mr. Hounslow is Secretary and Mr. Tolmaer is Vice President.

The N.B.F.A. is the international organization dedicated to the culture of this bird. They set and publish the standards, qualify the judges, organize the shows, award prizes, accept bird fanciers' clubs as affiliates and invite any individual who is interested to apply for membership. Write:

Hon. Secretary, Mr. E. J. Hounslow
N.B.F.A., 2 Bridge Street
Griffithstown
Gwent, South Wales, Great Britain

In the early 1950's most breeders of Bengalese found that it was almost impossible to get in the cards at shows when competing with most of the other common seedeaters such as the colorful waxbills and finches. It was therefore suggested that an effort should be made to get the Bengalese a class of their own.

This had already been done with the zebra finch only a few years earlier, and they were obviously going from strength to strength.

A notice was placed in *Cage Birds Magazine* advertising that there were thoughts of starting a specialist society for Bengalese, but the advertisement had very little response; only six people wrote to say that they were at all interested, and most of these came from various parts of the British Isles.

After consulting all the people who were known to have bred Bengalese, however, it was decided to try to form a society, regardless of the poor response to the advertisement. In the autumn of 1954 about ten people met in a huge disused and empty cinema in Tooting, South London. Those attending brought a motley selection of show cages containing their Bengalese.

After forming a committee, the first thing on the agenda was to settle the name of the bird. At that time there were three names in common use, Bengalese, Bengalee and Bengal finches, and occasionally they were referred to as the society finch, a name still frequently used in America today.

It was finally decided that the name should be Bengalese. A standard for the Bengalese was then established, and it remained unaltered for ten years. During this time tremendous strides were made by breeders in regard to both quality and size.

The first consideration was the type of bird to aim for. Most Bengalese at that time were rather thin in body, and it was decided to aim for a more cobby and rounded bird, more like the Border canary and with even markings such as chocolate with white wings or white head and tails, etc.

Colour was also considered, and a deep chocolate or rich fawn was to be the aim. As far as the crested variety was concerned, it was to be similar to the Gloster canary.

It should be borne in mind that at this time there were only two types in existence, the chocolate and white and the fawn and white. Crested birds were also available in both colors.

Having settled the standard, the next consideration was the type of show cage. Firstly the zebra finch show cage was considered, but as we had all seen these cages piled high on each other only to be knocked down, it was decided that this square type was not suitable.

Many other cage designs were discussed, and finally it was decided that we wanted a cage that:

    (a) could not be piled up

    (b) gave maximum light to the birds

    (c) was easy to construct, since we were entering the era of Do-It-Yourself.

The result was the Bengalese show cage which was easy to make from plywood and easy to equip with a front that could be made without a jig.

The fittings (e.g., strap hinges) could be easily bought. The water holder could be made from zinc or tin and bent to 1" diameter.

A rough set of rules was drawn up and after almost eight hours of discussion, often argument, the meeting was finally closed.

Cage & Aviary Birds Magazine reported extensively on this inaugural meeting, and this report resulted in quite a large increase in the number of members. During the first year the membership grew quite well; at the second meeting we were able to report that the membership had grown to 30.

We had been able to put on one or two classes at a few shows, mainly in the London area, as most of the members lived in or around the metropolis. At this time of course there were two classes, one for chocolate and white and fawn and white and the other for any other variety (A.O.V.) The entry was usually 10 to 12 in the first class and 3 or 4 in the second.

One of the main items on the agenda at this second annual meeting was whether we should amalgamate with the Zebra Finch Society, who were doing exceptionally well, or whether we should go it alone. By a very small majority we decided to go it alone. The N.B.F.A. has always been on very good terms with the Z.F.S., and one wonders what would have happened if the vote had gone the other way.

About this time, while assisting in a well known London bird establishment, we received an importation of mixed birds from Denmark. In the list accompanying the birds were 4 pairs of what was described as "Devil Finches"; on examination they were recognized as Bengalese, but they had a slight marking on the breast and had no white in their plumage. One bird died the following day, and it turned out that of the seven left 5 were cocks and 2 hens. Fortunately two pairs were bred and had a successful season, producing 15 young; 9 of these were hens.

Soon afterwards the late Mr. Watson of Fife in Scotland had a pair of almost self fawns, and with two self chocolates from the Danish stock he was the first person to breed self fawns.

In 1956 an approach was made to the National Exhibition of Cage Birds to put a class on for Bengalese; in fact they allowed us two classes, one for chocolate and white and fawn and white and one an A.O.V. class.

It may come as a surprise to many people that in 1956 we had 28 entries in the first class (choc./white, fawn/white) and two entries in the A.O.V. class. In 1957 there were ten entries in the A.O.V. class and in 1958 the A.O.V. class was 14.

Our membership had increased to almost 100 by 1960 and we had acquired very nice trophies for competition. In 1978 there were 70 organizations affiliated with the N.B.F.A.

Although we were always sure of a good entry at the national shows we did not seem to get many entries at local shows or patronage shows. This was partly due to the fact that very few judges of foreign birds were interested in Bengalese. Every effort was made to encourage their interest, even to sending them copies of the standard, but we met with little success.

An incident that happened might illustrate this. One of the pioneer Bengalese fanciers entered four pairs at one show, but on the day he was due to send the birds he was able to find only three good pairs. As four cages had been reserved and the carrying case was for four, he decided to send four cages anyway. Two pairs of birds were very good and one pair was good, but the fourth pair was terrible—the cock did not even have a tail. The result: No Tail won 1st, the good birds won 2nd and the two very good pairs got past the judge with a weak 6th and 7th.

The fancier was surprised at the result and wrote to the judge suggesting that there must be a mistake. His answer was that they were "only Bengalese" of which he knew nothing, so he had left one of the stewards to put the award labels on; these were stuck on the cages as they were lined up on the staging. Fortunately this doesn't happen these days, because more fanciers exhibit these birds, but the only way to get better judges and better classes for Bengalese is to show your birds. We are very fortunate that we have very few studs of Bengalese that always win, and very often the best Bengalese come from a Novice Exhibitor.

1

2

3

Now for the question "are your birds any good?" There is only one way to find out and that is to compare with others, and you can only do this by exhibiting them at shows. Then, if you are "well up" in the cards at two or more shows against competition, you can rest assured your birds are quite good. Good Bengalese are always in demand and will be worth much more than inferior birds. In these days of inflation we can well use the money that good stock realizes.

The advice to anyone just starting with Bengalese in the British Isles is to buy two or three pairs of good quality birds, preferably from an N.B.F.A. member, breed from these, band the young with Association closed rings, and exhibit them at one of the N.B.F.A. patronage shows. If they don't win you can always ask the judge, who will be an N.B.F.A. panel judge, why your birds are not placed. If you tell him that you are a beginner and wish to seek more knowledge, surely he will be only too pleased to advise you, especially if you ask in a polite manner.

If you cannot find the judge or he is busy, ask any of the champion exhibitors, as they will invariably always give you lots of advice. Exhibitors always feel proud to be asked their opinions.

1. Before buying finches, study them and compare them to the standards. If you are getting a poor quality bird, at least you should know it. 2. This gentleman in the Moscow bird market (an open-air affair), tried to sell this cage as a finch cage. It was unsuitable because the spacing between the wires was too large and the finches could squeeze through and escape. 3. A typical show cage for finches.

If you want to exhibit your finches, you must feed them a diet which is more than just a maintaining diet. Special supplements are necessary for the bird to grow to its maximum size and have its best colors showing. (Below) It is often helpful to keep finches together so you can compare them as to size and coloration.

Exhibiting

At most open shows held throughout the country there are usually separate classes for Bengalese. At one time Bengalese were included in the "Foreign" class, but most societies now provide separate classes although some still include Bengalese in the Foreign Seedeater section. The reason for separate classes being provided results from the work of the specialist society devoted to Bengalese and because many more people are breeding Bengalese for show; it's not like the old days, when Bengalese were kept solely for their role as foster parents.

It must be extremely difficult for a judge to judge birds that have a standard against birds that do not have one, and perhaps the day will come when separate classes for Bengalese will be provided at all shows.

The standards laid down by the N.B.F.A. are as follows:

Type Is Paramount to Color
Standard of Color

Chocolate/White Pairs: Markings are immaterial but should be matched as near as possible on each bird.

Fawn/White Pairs: Markings are immaterial but should be matched as near as possible on each bird.

Chocolate Self Pairs: Head, wings, tail and half way down the breast to be dark chocolate, the lower half of the breast to be light chocolate, with or without fleckings also on the center of the back. No white feathers are permissible.

Fawn Self Pairs: Head, wings, tail and half way down the breast to be dark fawn, the lower half of the breast to be light fawn, with or without fleckings also on the center of the back. No white feathers are permissible.

White Self Pairs: The whole of the birds are to be white, both birds are to have the same eye color. No fawn or chocolate feathers are permissible.

Dilute Chocolate/White Pairs: Feather color to be pale chestnut and white. Beak to be steel gray upper—lighter lower. Leg color to be pinky white to light gray.

Dilute Fawn/White Pairs: White background with diffused pastel fawn. Eye to be pink and prominent. Beak to be light steel gray to pink. Leg color to be pink to pale gray.

Crests: Balance of color is not important with the crested. The aim is to try to match your pairs as near as possible, get the crest as large and as near a single crest as possible. To be shown as one crested and one non-crested.

Beaks and Legs: Beaks and legs on all mutations should match as near as possible.

Feature	Standard
WINGS	Compact, set close to body, just meeting at tips (15 points).

BODY	Nicely rounded, neck thick, head round from tip of beak to nape of neck, as little neck as possible. Beak in proportion to size of head, eyes set well back from base of beak. Back slightly rounded. No undue fatness. (20 points).
TAIL	Straight, clean, no loose feathers (10 points).
CONDITION	Judged with feather quality (20 points).
POSITION	Approximately 45 degrees (15 points).
PAIRS, MATCHING AND MARKINGS	Pair to consist of cock and hen of same color. Crest to be shown as a pair of the same color, one with crest and one without crest. Preference to birds with similar markings. Additional points for evenly marked birds (20 points).

Note that the color standards begin with the statement: "Type is paramount to color."

THE STANDARD BENGALESE SHOW CAGE
Specification

Size Overall: 13¼" long x 10½" high x 5" wide

Top, Sides, False Roof and Bottom: Solid

Back: 4 mm. ply

Front Rail: 1¾" from floor

Wire Front: 26 wires, 16 gauge, ½" centers: double punched bars at top, set ½" apart for strength: cross bar level with perches or 2" from bottom bar. (3 wires extended top and bottom for fixing).

Top: Width 2 5/8" with carrying hole 1¼" dia. centered 1" from back of cage.

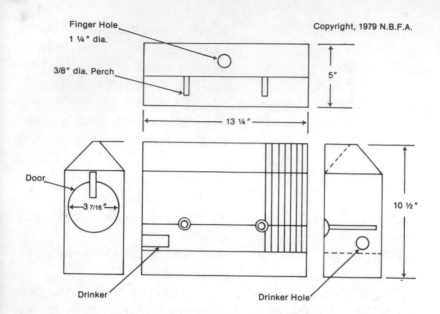

Copyright, 1979 N.B.F.A.

The standard show cage approved by the National Bengalese Fanciers Association.

Door: Round, 3½" dia. centered 5¼" from bottom of cage with One Brass Strap Hinge 2" x ¼" open

Perches: Length 4" overall: plain boss at back 1" dia. projecting 1/8": fixed 4" from floor of cage and 3¾" from sides.

Drinker: 2½" long x 1¼" dia. of zinc or tinplate with open top, painted white: with wire guard 1¼" x 1¼" with center bar.

Drinker Hole: 1¼" dia. centered 2" from bottom of cage, 1 5/8" from side: situated on left-hand side of cage. Wire guard pushes up when drinker is replaced and also stops bird getting into water pot.

Color: Matt white inside: glossy black outside: black bars.

Birds may be exhibited in standard zebra finch show cages or in Bengalese show cages.

40

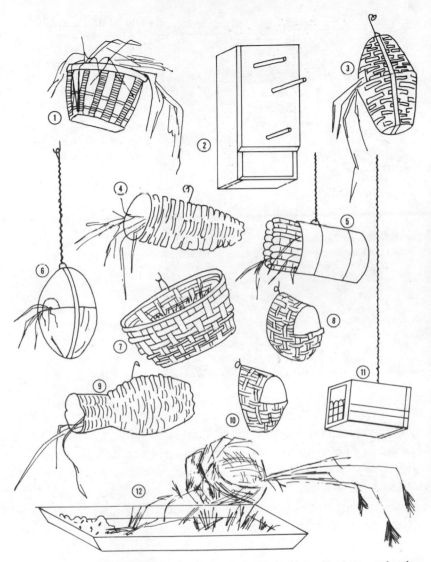

Various nests and roosts used by both society finches and zebra finches in the author's indoor aviary. Most of the nests are of the wicker-type construction available at pet shops, but some (2, 5, 6, 11) are homemade. Not all nests were equally favored by both species. # 6, for example, a halved coconut shell held together with rubber bands and suspended from the ceiling, is very popular with zebra finches but is ignored by societies. # 12 is a society ground nest built within a rooted clump of rye grass that had been stuffed into a deep water dish. Drawing by Mimi Rickel.

The author's aviary for finches was merely a converted room with the windows double-screened. One of the author's greatest joys (below) is to handfeed his chicks so they accept him as "mother" and quickly come to perch on his finger and beg for food.

Getting Started

Build up steam slowly. Most fanciers who have continued to enjoy their birds over the decades started slowly. They made fewer mistakes and made those mistakes with fewer birds.

Ideally, you started with a book, this book perhaps. Hopefully you will at least skim through it once before you spend any big money. More likely you already have purchased one or two society finches and a cage for them. Good! Stop! Take your birds into your home and enjoy them with a minimum of paraphernalia and remedies, at least until you begin to soak in the full flavor of your purchase.

Watch your birds one or two days. Would you rather have whites, pieds, selfs, dilutes, with or without crests? Perhaps you favor uniformity. It will be easier to exchange two birds than twenty. The general care, caging, habits, longevity and even cost are very much different regardless of what you choose. The range of prices from the most ordinary pied chocolate to the pure white crested is only

A pair of finches sitting on their eggs. This was a strobelight picture taken at night, when the birds were sleeping. Photo by Harry Lacey.

about as one is to two. Compare that range of prices with give-away mongrel dogs versus $10,000 Westminster Kennel Club champions.

If you have not yet bought the cage, try to find one with three-eighths inch wire spacing. The more common half-inch gap will hold adult society finches, but juveniles and other finch species you may later acquire just might get between bars with half-inch spacing, especially if the bars are thin and unsupported for long distances. Cage design will be covered in more detail later, but this advice, for starters, might save you some sadness later.

Situate the cage where it is not subject to drafts, not liable to be knocked by a swinging door, not under a bright light that is frequently turned on and off, not where a dog or a cat can make the birds miserable or worse.

A bedroom is perfectly appropriate. The birds will sleep when the people sleep. A cloth cage cover is not usually necessary. If the cage is in a corner where drafts are not going to chill the birds, then there is certainly no need to cover them at night, but it's always wise to have a cover handy anyway.

Your society finches will get along well with many other small cage birds. If you want variety in a large cage you could keep them with, for example, cordon bleus, red-ears, orange-cheeks, lavenders, Gouldians, green singing finches and zebra finches. Societies are sociable. They eat much the same food as all those mentioned above and perhaps twenty other popular caged finches as well.

The big problem you will be faced with in the first few months with your birds is to resist becoming the owner of more than you can comfortably house. If you enjoy your first cageful of society finches it might be a good idea to shift gears before you buy another cage or another bird. Instead, subscribe to a cage bird magazine, join a club, attend a show, broaden your vista, see what the other fellow is doing—there will always be more birds for you to buy.

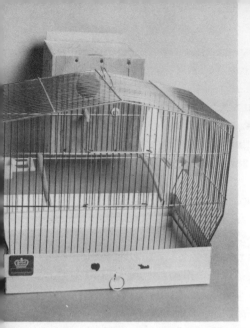

The cage you select to house your society finches can be an inexpensive small beginner's cage or a large converted room (below), which was the author's choice.

Cages

Cages for society finches can be ornate or utilitarian. Some popular cages obviously have been designed for economy of cleaning and feeding effort, and still others feature economy of construction or economy of space. If you slice the pie thinly enough you would do better with a stuffed bird or a carving or a really good photograph.

If you desire, caging can become an architectural or decorative part of your home. A large cage can be created to serve as a room divider. Remember, as you plan such a project, that you will need to remove birds, feed and water them and furnish bath facilities and perching accommodations. You might opt for potted plants as perches; if so, you should make the door large enough to get those plants in and out.

Partitions and enclosures for the birds are traditionally made of wire mesh or metal rods, but raffia or strips of bamboo also provide security, and in certain decorative schemes they prove especially attractive. Glass is easy to look through but of course doesn't permit circulation of air, and it also mutes any sounds. If parallel walls are close together—say no more than eighteen inches apart—the risk of injury to a bird by flying into a transparent window is not great. For one thing, your birds will quickly learn to do most of their flying the "long" way, and also it would be hard even for a society finch to pick up much speed in these narrow confines. Fortunately, society finches are not highstrung; they do well in confinement.

Some zoos have mastered the technique of "caging" birds by means of curtain walls of fast-moving currents of air. This may seem a bit sophisticated for even a modern home, but we do have central vacuum systems in many houses today, and central air conditioning fans operate around the clock. But remember the problems with drafts!

Birds tend to fly horizontally, so they travel more horizontal distance than vertical distance in the course of a lifetime. If you have space and money for three cubic feet of cage, it would be better three feet long by a foot high and a foot wide than three feet high and a foot square on the base.

The cage previously suggested is large enough for one pair to breed or for four birds to live together wholesomely. If you can provide a larger home for your pets, so much the better. Flying is good for them, and maintenance is easier in larger quarters.

If you have direct sunlight available, this is great. Just remember not to let the sun cook your pets. They should always have some place in the cage or aviary where they can roost in the shade. They should also have cool, fresh bath water before them at least whenever they are exposed to the sun. One aspect of sunlight relates to the ultraviolet radiation present in unfiltered sunlight. This is the range of wavelengths which, when directed on certain oils and fats, creates vitamin D. Now vitamin D is vital in all bony creatures, since calcium cannot be assimilated without it. No vitamin D, no hard egg shells, no strong bones. Simple as that. This is why we drink milk (high in calcium) that has been irradiated by ultraviolet to produce vitamin D. If you pass sunlight through window glass, most of the ultraviolet is absorbed by the glass. The bird is able to generate its own vitamin D if it gets sufficient exposure to unfiltered sunlight. You can design your caging to provide direct exposure to sunlight, or you can feed vitamin D supplements. Both methods work perfectly; take your choice.

Buy an anodized aluminum or stainless steel or chromium plated cage if you can afford it. In the long run these cages will be the least expensive. Galvanized steel mesh is also durable, but it's less attractive in the home. A canary cage or a budgie cage will house a society finch as well, but if you have a choice, choose the cage designed for the society finches—eventually you may wish to breed societies, and then a large long cage will make a fine breeding establishment.

If you plan on an aviary, wonderful! Society finches do well in them, especially if they are planted with tough plants. A tender leaf will end up on the floor. Try potted fruit trees, forsythia and privets. Be sure you have buried galvanized wire mesh deeply around your on-the-ground aviary to keep out rats, mice, weasels, cats and other vermin and predators.

As mentioned before, the ideal screening is mesh 3/8" square; 3/8" by 1" will do also. Most adult societies will not get through a ½" x 1" opening, but juveniles might—so might some of the smaller finches you may acquire, and young mice can certainly get through ½" x 1"—perhaps even ½" x ½". All bird keepers agree that 3/8" spacing keeps all birds in and all mammals out.

Incidentally, mice are not predators. They don't bite the

49

birds, but nevertheless they can cause the birds to die. Mice are nocturnal and society finches are diurnal, so the societies (which are caged and unable to get away) will be kept awake until they waste away from lack of sleep. Mice also foul the grain.

The cage or aviary should have provisions for food, drinking water, bathing water, grits, perching, nesting (if this is what you have in mind) and a place to hang a cuttlebone. Not too difficult or costly when you consider the pleasure these birds will provide.

CAGE HINTS

Don't confine birds too closely. Give them room to stretch and exercise—one dimension of the cage should be not less than 24 inches—preferably more like 36"—and this should be a horizontal dimension. For a rough rule of thumb, as you get started, do not exceed two birds per cubic foot of cage space. Don't crowd them. Give each of your birds a home it can call its own. In other words, don't crowd them for the sake of owning one more color variety or crest or just one more bird.

Set up double feeding and double watering facilities. Then if you are away for a day you will not have misgivings, and your birds will not suffer. Also, if a bully turns up (unlikely, but possible), the others in the cage will at least be able to eat while the bully is eating.

Feed only the quantity of fresh soft supplements that the caged birds will clean up in an hour. This is especially important with hard-boiled eggs and fresh greens.

You should have an isolation cage for any new acquisitions. Don't assume that an antibiotic is equal to quarantine. This is not so. There is no universal remedy. Furthermore, antibiotics frequently wipe out *all* the bacteria in the alimentary canal—including the "good" ones. You may cure a disease with a "one shot" treatment but then cause a bird to starve even with a gizzard full of grain because the normal "good" bacteria in the intestines that facilitate digestion have been wiped out by the antibiotic along with the "bad" biota.

Try to provide perches of various diameters and shapes. Grasping a variety of shapes and sizes is good for the feet. Also, do not use perches with sand on them, but rather watch your birds and if necessary clip their nails just long enough to miss the blood vessel. In some situations your birds will go for years without needing a nail clipping.

AVIARY HINTS

If you are going to be away for a few days and want to reduce the risks and problems for your bird sitter, set up a few quarts of water in inverted bottles. The screw-on covers are all you must buy and are available in pet shops and feed stores. They are especially intended for chicks and pigeons but nevertheless are great for finches. The jars are ordinary canning jars or mayonnaise jars—most housewives have a few in a cupboard or on a basement shelf.

If you must catch one particular bird in an aviary, go after it quietly at night with a flashlight if you know where it roosts. Most birds roost in the same place every night. If that system is not applicable, use a net and remember that the best time to swing the net is at *the moment the bird lands.* Once it is settled, it has begun to think out its escape routes, but as it alights it is not as prepared to take off, and so your chances of making a painless capture are improved.

If you are letting your birds breed you should decide whether you will leave them strictly alone for the four or five weeks from nest-building to weaning the fledglings *or* whether you should visit and inspect them every day. *Either* system works, but you may get a deserted nest if you start fooling around for the first time after the nest has gone two or three weeks with no human interference. The birds really don't *need* you, and you really don't *need* to do anything for them unless you plan to apply closed bands to the week-old babies.

You may not wish to breed your birds, so you might reasonably assume that no nests are necessary. This is not entirely correct, since many finches (including societies and zebras), especially young birds, will prefer to gather at night in a nest rather than perch on a dowel or a twig. Hang a small wicker nest with a front opening (or an open cup) in the cage and you may find that your birds jam themselves into it at night, getting packed in like sardines. Good! Let them.

If your birds are scary, try a dim night light. You may save a valuable bird from breaking its neck against a window or a screen.

If your birds are scary, search out the culprit—sometimes a rodent or a cat or a hawk flying outside or over the aviary. Give your captive birds hiding places—shrubs, bundles of brush or twigs—something to pop into; a privet hedge bush is good because it is bright green all year and is neither poisonous nor thorny.

SUN BATHS

Sunbathing is a form of bathing your societies will indulge in whenever the opportunity affords. Really, they are very busy "doing things" all the daylight hours, but they are opportunists and when the sun shines, they will spread their feathers and soak in some sun rays. If the sunlight gets to your birds through a glass window it will have lost that vitally important ingredient, ultraviolet but the birds will still enjoy it.

"Oiling" is still another activity engaged in by society finches. Your society finch has a fatty gland at the base of its tail that it can reach with its bill. The gland is stimulated by rubbing to secrete oil; with its bill, the bird distributes the oil over its feathers. This tends to waterproof them, but the exact reason why society finches do it is not positively known—it may serve to preserve body heat.

LIGHTING

The length of the day may determine the birds' enthusiasm for nesting. You might opt for an extended "daylight" period and assure it by use of a clock timer which causes a light to go on at perhaps 3 A.M. or 4 A.M. or 5 A.M. and remain on until just after sun-up. A degree of brightness to read a newspaper by is sufficient at these early times. People create this extension of daylight with chickens *all the time*, as a matter of course. It is well established as a technique in aviculture. You should avoid any schedule of artificial light which causes darkness to fall suddenly on the birds. If they are *suddenly* deprived of *all* light they will not be able to find their roosting places.

Your birds are naturally diurnal. They naturally sleep at night and are active during the light hours. Actually, they will begin to roost for the night an hour before dusk. The young are fed intermittently during the day only, and it is your job to give the birds the peace and quiet they are accustomed to at night.

This is important especially for breeders. If a setting adult is kicked off the eggs at night (generally the male sets at night), and it is really dark, it may not find its way back and the eggs or fledglings will take a chill—perhaps a fatal chill.

So plan your day around the natural habits of the birds and get the chores completely done at least one hour before dusk. A very dim light in (or close to) the aviary at night may be of value if the birds are scary. A 10-watt lamp in a 100-square-foot room is ample, and 7½ watts would probably suffice to help a disturbed bird find its way back to its customary roosting place. Ten watts for one hundred hours equals one kilowatt hour—and that costs less than ten cents per week if it is left on for 15 hours daily between dusk and dawn. If you have birds in a large cage or aviary, this night light might well be mounted under a large pie-pan-shaped reflector; it will then also provide a little warmth for sick or weak birds. An overly cold cage will be obvious if all the birds—otherwise healthy—cluster under this light. Ideally, for society finches the nights should be dark, warm, and quiet.

TEMPERATURE

Many excellent English language books which contain information about society finches were written by Englishmen for bird keepers who live in England. Aviaries are usually described in some detail and outdoor flights are covered too. The English authors assume that all this bird-keeping will be taking place between the English Channel and the Scottish border. This is a matter of about six degrees of latitude from 50° N. to 56° N.

There are very few places in Canada or the U.S. where the climate is exactly the same. To begin with, there is hardly a place in England which is more than 100 miles from the sea. This tempers the climate. Summers are cooler than in Alberta or North Dakota, and winters are warmer than in Oklahoma. The average temperature in the south of England is 52° F. and only four degrees cooler at the northern Scottish border. In the coldest month (January) the mean temperature is 40° F. It is foggy or cloudy for 2/3 of the time that the sun is above the horizon. So, when you read a book about aviculture written by an Englishman while you are in an armchair in Milton, Wisconsin, Salem, West Virginia, or Alfred, New York, you should consider the source of your information.

Outdoor aviaries in southern California, Gulf Coast Texas, Mississippi, Louisiana, Florida and other warm areas are probably O.K. for society finches all twelve months of the year if some protection against rare frosts is provided in the form of roosting boxes or access to a closed structure adjacent to the outdoor flight.

As you get north (or inland) more protection against frost is required, and the screened flight will not be useful for as many months of the year. There is no sense in going too far with this, because we all know that a southern exposure of a house or the southeast side of a hill can easily be ten degrees warmer than another spot only a few hundred yards away. Just bear in mind that society finches are semi-tropical birds—domesticated for centuries, but still not as rugged as a Plymouth Rock chicken. Use your intelligence. If they look cold, give them more warmth. If they look well and happy, you must be doing something right.

There are very few absolutes in nature, so there is no absolutely ideal temperature for your birds. A cool morning may be stimulating to your finches, but a continuously cold aviary will kill or weaken them; certainly it will stifle their desire to breed. A daily range of 60° to 85° F. (15.6° to 29.4° C) is a good safe point of departure. Anything less than 45° F., and that only for short periods, could cause a disaster. Surely there are successful breeders in Florida whose birds tolerate many summer days at well over 85° F. Also, you will, if you remain in this hobby, eventually meet or hear about a breeder in Scotland or Germany (or is it Siberia?) who succeeded although his aviary never got up to 65° F. This book, though, is intended to help you set up wholesome situations, not marginal procedures.

Cold drafts and prolonged cold rains are to be avoided. An aviary that is screened on top and sides is perfectly all right; in fact it is an added "plus," but no cagebird should be forced to remain exposed to stiff, cold, wet winds. Be sure that there is ample shelter for all your birds at all times. It is true that society finches will enjoy bathing in cool water, but they will do best if they can dry out quickly on a warm draft-free perch, preferably in direct sunlight.

Three society finch chicks peering out of their nest. They soon will be ready to leave the nest. The photo below shows the same chicks at eight days of age. Breeding society finches provides income as well as entertainment.

Breeding

Experienced bird keepers advise novices to begin to breed their birds at eight months of age. This is good advice. It takes a lot out of a bird, especially a hen, to manufacture five or so hard-shelled eggs and then skip most of her social activities for a month and a half. Let her mature fully and gain her own strong bones before commencing this major project. This is good advice for bird keepers, but unfortunately society finches don't cotton to advice from humans and, if left to their own devices, may do what comes naturally at perhaps four months of age. If you don't want them to breed, first figure out which are the boys and which are the girls and then separate the sexes. Males, females, and juveniles all look just about alike, but:

Males build nests.

Males sing to females.

Males sing at each other.

Males hop about with stems of grass in their bills.

Males puff their belly feathers and stretch their necks.

Males lower their heads and bounce about.

Females don't do any of those things.

Buy colored plastic open bands in several colors and use them to identify sexes and pairs.

Then, when you are ready, let your birds breed, and they will, 12 months of the year, if they have good nutrition, light, warmth, rest at night and a place to do their thing.

The place is a nest box or a basket approximately 4½ inches cubed. Don't be surprised if all the best advice you get suggests covered top boxes and then your birds choose an open canary type basket—it looks like the sieve used in a household kitchen for sifting cake flour.

The male will fill the box or basket or sieve with grass, leaves, twigs, stems, rags, thread, string, cotton and paper while the female lays her eggs. She will begin to lay about ten days after they copulate and will probably lay five eggs over the course of six or so days. The birds may begin to incubate the eggs after the fourth has been laid. The male will probably set at night and the female during the day, but he may spell her during the day so that she can get some food and water. At night they may both set on the eggs, or he may build a second nest for sitting, not to be confused with setting. He will remain busy during the day adding material to the already overcrowded nest.

The eggs will darken after three or four days of incubation and should hatch with no help from you after twelve to fourteen days. Hopefully, all that are going to hatch will hatch at about the same time. If one is a day or two late, it will probably be crowded by its nestmates and will end up as a runt if it should manage to survive.

The parents may not begin to feed the nestlings until

about ten hours after they hatch—or until sunrise of the following day. Don't worry; this is how they do it.

Nestlings will grow rapidly and after about four weeks they will be gone from the nest, looking much like their parents, but with shorter tails.

During this period of raising the chicks your birds should get food supplementary to the regular water, grits, millet, canary seed and greens. The supplements can be soaked and sprouted seeds if you haven't been feeding them previously, nestling foods available from your pet shop, whole wheat bread soaked in milk, hard-boiled egg or scrambled egg pulverized through a strainer. It really isn't difficult, but as you refine your techniques you will discover that there are many additional things you can do to improve fertility and egg-shell quality, reduce mortality and turn out bigger, healthier chicks. This specialized information is in itself sufficient to fill a book.

A drawing in this book (p. 41) shows one screened wall of an aviary for society and zebra finches. There were nineteen adult birds in this enclosure, which measures eight by twelve feet. A window (not shown) opens to a screened outdoor flight which is used in warm weather.

Notice the tray on the floor; it holds sprouting millet. This is where the bath water and the hulls of grain are dumped. The dirty bath water wets and fertilizes the soil for the uneaten seed, which sprouts to provide fresh green food throughout the year.

Between the tray and the wall there is another plastic container. This had been placed there to hold a handful of garden weeds. Their stems and roots are in an inch or two of water in that container. Notice also that there are about a half-dozen really nice nest baskets hanging on the screen. Now, in direct contradiction to all the "rules" we make about society finches, there on the floor is a nest, built by three male society finches and containing seven eggs, incubated by all six parents more or less—sometimes three birds at a time incubating. These three pairs had six baskets to choose from. Other birds (later) did establish nests in several of these baskets, and they too are successfully raising their young in these more conventional arrangements. But down on the floor is that basket-shaped, basketless nest, built entirely by three male society finches in a clump of *damp* weeds. Could it have been the dampness that attracted these birds?

SECURITY

The word "security" as applied to society finches covers several different areas of concern. In no special order, please consider enemies, escapes and pests.

Enemies include wild birds, mice, rats, cats and small boys. A young mouse, for instance, can sometimes squeeze through half-inch screening and, by scurrying around at night, rob your birds of sleep and even cause them to hurt themselves as they blindly fly into objects at night. Should you wish to propagate your birds they will not successfully produce maximum clutches if they are harassed at night by mice or other creatures. You must assure them of a quiet night, every night.

Make up your mind before you invest too much cash or time—do you wanted to breed birds or simply show them off to all comers—smokers, coughers, sneezers, cage rattlers, shouters, photographers and arm-wavers included.

Escapes are easy for society finches. They are inquiring, probing and searching all the day long. If an opening one inch in diameter exists anywhere, they will find it and be out even if they didn't really want to go anywhere in particular. If you build an aviary, make the doors as low as you can conveniently bend under. Many escapes take place over your head when a high door is opened. Corridors and arrangements of double doors are ideal for prevention of escapes. The trouble is that you have to open and close twice as many doors in order to make a visit.

BATHING

Society finches love to bathe. To watch them rattle their wings and tails in a shallow dish of water is to watch birds in bliss. It is obvious to anyone who witnesses these ablutions that these birds are not acting out of duty or boredom or instinct but because they seem to take pleasure in splashing. When one jumps in, the others will follow, and for about five minutes pandemonium prevails. A spray of water swamps the area for several feet in every direction.

The birds will wet themselves to a point just short of where flying becomes difficult, and then they will flit off to a perch (preferably in bright sunlight) for drying, fluffing and preening. They surely will go through this routine once daily; some birds will do it twice if clean cool water is available. The ideal water depth seems to be about one-half inch, and ordinary fresh clean tap water is all they want or need.

The bathing accomplishes several things. It probably helps control lice. It carries off dirt and dead particles of skin and feathers. It moistens the feathers of birds that are incubating eggs, and this moisture aids in the hatching process. When eggs with live embryos don't hatch, the fault is frequently with the moisture. Bear in mind that nests in cages don't get the benefit of rain or even the morning dew.

You may substitute a spray in a planted aviary or an outside flight for the bath dish. Better still, offer both. For a bird without webbed feet, it is really surprising how much societies demonstrate their enjoyment of clean, fresh, cool water.

Chlorine is frequently added to municipal water supplies to reduce odors and also to reduce the possibility of disease transmission. Some birds tolerate small amounts of chlorine, but others seem to resent it. Fortunately, chlorine escapes to the air if water is left standing with a large surface exposed. Agitation helps. Boiling also helps but is really unnecessary.

If your water is heavily chlorinated, simply draw off what you need into gallon plastic milk bottles. Fill only up to the level where the neck of the bottle begins (say three quarts) and let it stand, uncorked, for a day or two. Hot tap water will give up chlorine even faster. Let it stand until it cools, then use it.

Water temperature is not an issue with society finches. Serve it at room temperature or cooler; it will soon warm up to room temperature regardless. Same goes for drinking water. Since societies will bathe twice daily if you leave water out for them, an anodized aluminum rustproof cage earns its keep. Generally the tray or the bottom of the cage gets most of the punishment from grits, mineral grits, bird droppings and water.

ZEBRAS AND SOCIETIES

If you already have had some experience with zebra finches or if you plan to keep zebras and societies in the same aviary or large cage, there are just a few points to keep in mind.

Societies cannot tolerate the low temperatures that don't bother a zebra. For example, zebra finches will nest and raise young in aviaries in which the water freezes every night. This is also brought to mind when you examine their nests. Zebra finches weave feathers into their nests when they are available, but under the same conditions society finches will construct nests solely of twigs, stems and leaves. Also, zebra finches are more prone to nest in a whole coconut shell or a covered box, while society finches will more likely choose the open cup.

Both species are millet eaters and avid bathers. Neither species is especially interested in live insect food, but both will eat fresh greens, hard-boiled eggs and sometimes fresh fruits such as apples.

Society finches make better foster parents, but zebras

produce more of their own young, as witness the prices in the marketplace: common zebras are less expensive than common societies.

Both species have the same cage-size requirements. They usually ignore each other but will eat and bathe side-by-side.

Baby zebras make rasping noises and baby societies make squeaking noises when they beg for food.

In the British Isles each species has its own fancier association and each association specifies its own standard show cage. Recently the National Bengalese Fancier Society (N.B.F.A.) announced that their members' birds could be exhibited and judged in *either* the standard N.B.F.A. cage *or* in a standard Zebra Finch Society show cage.

VISITORS

It is a good idea to be close to your society finches. Visit them daily—during the light hours. If you breed a few, handle the babies once their eyes are open, if only to get bands on them. Society finches have been with people for a long time and seem, instinctively, to get along well with us. They will not become as intimate with you as a budgie or a parrot, but as you watch your birds you will notice that you are trusted. We have learned—and birds know instinctively—that they are vulnerable when they bathe. It is not easy to take off from a muddy or wet surface, and it is not possible to fly at top speed with wet feathers. Nevertheless, your societies will bathe while you watch them. Under similar circumstances a cordon bleu or an orange-checked waxbill would be less likely to bathe with someone hovering nearby.

Cagebirds do well with routine. Create a routine and then try to live with it. Cage cleaning, feeding, nest inspection and casual visits should all be during the bright light hours, regardless of whether the light is daylight or artificial.

Don't let daylight dim and then suddenly turn on brilliant electric lights and expect your birds to appreciate your company. Societies will probably tolerate the shock, but other species of finches could easily keel over after a few such experiences.

Noise is also a problem you will have to cope with. Again, your birds will adjust to conditions that build up gradually and then repeat themselves at predictable intervals. Look at birds and bats in a belfry. Every hour on-the-hour a two-ton bronze bell is struck by a hundred-pound cast iron hammer, and all day long the bats sleep through it and all night long the birds sleep through it. And on Sunday morning at ten or eleven o'clock, pandemonium breaks loose; yet these animals come back day after day, for generations. *Routine* disturbances are really not disturbances.

If you breed your birds (and this is not especially difficult), decide early on that you will either look in the nest once daily every day or stay strictly away for the entire six weeks from first egg to flying fledgling. These precautionary notes will be no great imposition on you—but if you are aiming to take that step from owning a cage of birds to becoming a bird keeper, this is how to begin. Here is where we separate the men from the boys, the sheep from the goats, the bird owners from the bird keepers.

Zebra finches are very popular and easy to breed. They are excellent cage-mates for society finches, too. Three varieties of zebra finches are shown here (left to right): fawn, normal and a pair of whites.

A chick is best fed by its mother! But you can hand-feed it, too. The author stores the seed in a plastic bottle inside the aviary. As he requires seed, he merely pours it into the seed tray.

Food

Your society finch is an easy bird to satisfy. It needs millet, water, minerals and vitamins. It should have grits for the gizzard to utilize in order to grind grain, but it will probably survive a long time without the grit. Chickens and pigeons fed on mash live out their lives without grit, although the reason for not providing it to them is not applicable to society finches. The minerals required by your society finches can be incorporated in the grit mixture or in other food supplements available from your pet shop. The vitamins not present in millet are found in hard-boiled eggs, cod liver oil, fresh raw vegetation (including spinach, carrot tops, grass cuttings, sprouted grain) or again in supplements available from your pet dealer. You pay your money and you take your choice.

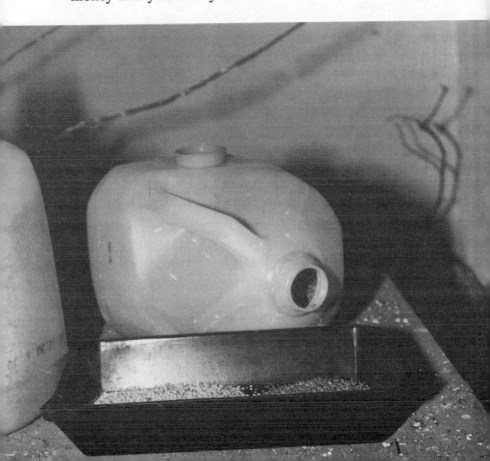

This goes also for the millet—society finches will eat 100% red millet or 100% spray millet, or they'll eat a mixture of various millets mixed further with canary, rape, poppy, flax, niger, hulled oats or a commercial finch mixture. The seed you offer should be alive and capable of sprouting if you plant it. It should not be smelly, moldy or damp, nor should it have been sprayed with insecticide. It should be free from mouse and wild bird droppings. It should look clean and bright regardless of whether it is a mixture or just one type of millet supplemented by just one seed of high fat and high protein content.

Your birds will pinch the grains between the upper and lower bill one at a time, and the husk will pop off and be dropped. The hulled grain is then swallowed, stored in the crop, ground in the gizzard and digested. You should check the grain supply frequently.

One pitfall experienced by many beginning finch keepers is the pitfall of husks versus seeds. These birds don't carry whole seeds in their bills, and they don't swallow them either. When a society finch picks up a grain of canary seed (*Phalaris canarius*) or a grain of millet (*Setaria italica* or *Panicum milaceum*), it positions and holds the grain between the upper and lower bill, using its tongue to manipulate it. A squeeze or two pops the husk off in one or two parts and then the husked seed is swallowed. The husk falls aside within an inch of the place it was picked up. Soon the seed dispenser or dish is full of inedible chaff and the birds could be starving. If your eyes are not sharp enough to discriminate between whole grain and husks, you might try blowing at the food dish. Since the chaff will be much lighter and since it is cup-shaped, it will tend to be caught in the air stream and carried off. If you keep several hundred birds you should buy a winnower; it will pay for itself in saved grain, and you can give up blowing before you are worn out.

An alternative to winnowing is to dump the chaff-laden

grain in a tray of moistened earth. The chaff will become mulch, and much of the remaining grain will sprout. Your birds will then consume in sprouted form what would otherwise be lost.

The following list was derived from the companion book *Breeding Society Finches* and other sources. The values for seeds are for *whole* seeds. When they have their husks removed, the fiber content goes down and the percentages of the remaining components go up commensurately.

Notice that canary seed is unusually high in minerals (ash), but also be aware that these figures will vary with the soil in which the plants are growing, the rainfall and the maturity of the seeds when they were harvested. The bird seed business is well established and highly competitive. Generally, you get what you pay for.

Many finches enjoy supplements to their diet in the form of cooked rice, the yolks of hard-boiled eggs, crumbled and scattered, and, of course, the usual diet of small seeds.

Foodstuff	Protein	Fat	Fiber	Ash	Carbo-hydrate, other than fiber
Egg (White)	10%	1	0	1	0
Egg (Yolk)	15	24	0	1	0
Bread	16	2	2	2	70
Green Vegetables Mostly leafy— varies greatly with moisture	10	3	25	1	20
Peanut Butter	30	40	3	2	15
Rice	8	2	9	5	65
Millet	13	2	9	4	62
Canary Seed	14	4	21	10	27
Spray Millet	15	6	11	6	51
Sunflower	15	28	29	3	17
Fennel	16	12	14	9	32
Niger	19	43	14	3	12
Rape	20	45	6	4	18
Caraway	20	17	16	7	29
Poppy	21	50	5	7	10
Sesame	21	47	5	6	19
Hemp	22	30	19	5	16
Gold of Pleasure	22	31	11	7	22
Flax	24	37	6	4	22

There is no shortage of customers willing to buy spray millet for their birds at prices *over* two dollars per pound, and in small quantities even three dollars a pound! They know that their birds love it.

Release your birds in a large aviary and let them settle down. Some will bathe, others will roost; still others will pick at grits, preen, build nests or fly back and forth. There will be little or no uniform activity, especially if there are several species present. Then put a few stalks of spray millet in a weighted vase or hang a bundle from a wire and within minutes *all* the birds of *all* the species will be picking over that millet.

VITAMINS

As we go down the list don't let it frighten you. A diversified diet will probably provide all the vitamins your birds will ever need, and a vitamin supplement from your pet dealer will be guaranteed to provide these substances. Just for the record, here are their names, natural sources and the diseases of birds which develop when the vitamins are absent.

Vitamin A—Found in eggs and green vegetables, it improves night vision and resistance to infection, especially of the skin. It is possible that excessive dosing of vitamin A causes French molt in budgies.

Vitamin B—This is the famous beri-beri nerve disease vitamin. Actually there are a dozen or so vitamin B complexes associated mostly with proteins and yeast.

Vitamin C—This is the citrus fruit vitamin. Also called ascorbic acid. Seed-eating birds seem to manufacture it and so do not require any in their diet.

Vitamin D—Calcium metabolism depends on vitamin D; its source is ultraviolet radiation on some oils and fats. Birds in direct sunlight make their own vitamin D.

Vitamin E—Found in seed germs, it is destroyed through oxidation by excessive dosage of cod liver oil.

Vitamin K—Required for coagulation of blood. Produced in the intestines by bacteria and so not required in the diet. Especially vulnerable to antibiotics.

Niacin—Vital for growth and good plumage, it is associated with proteins.

Biotin—Improves egg hatchability.

Vitamins A, D, E and K are soluble in fats and are often associated with edible oils or fats. Vitamin B and C are soluble in water.

It is entirely possible that indiscriminate dosing of cagebirds with antibiotics can actually destroy vitamins or reduce the ability of the bird to assimilate the vitamins it does ingest.

SUPPLEMENTS TO THE BASIC DIET

After the basic millet, grit and water, the sky is the limit with society finches. As long as you don't deprive your birds of those basic items, you can add anything that you think they might need or might like. These birds will not overeat, nor will they go off on dietary toots. For starters you might try any of the following and then branch out as your imagination or convenience directs. Try, for example:

Spray millet. This is expensive but it is a favorite food of all small seed-eating birds.

Weed seeds, rape, niger, cracked peanuts and cracked sunflower seeds are all eaten to some extent.

Green grasses, sprouts, carrot tops and spinach are high in vitamin A and other nutrient substances.

Mealworms and insectile food are sometimes taken, especially by youngsters.

Sprouted seed is soaked seed that has germinated over the course of three or four days. The husks are opened. It is especially useful a a food supplement for young birds and nestlings.

Bread, bread soaked in milk or water, stale bread, bread crumbs, toasted bread, buttered toast, toast and peanut butter, cracker meal and wheat germ are all excellent food supplements.

Some finches will peck at a piece of raw apple.

TWO DIET DON'TS

Don't leave any uneaten food which may sour or become rancid.

Don't substitute these foods for the basic diet; instead supplement the basic diet with these and anything similar. Also bear in mind that supplements are not treats. Supplements *should supplement* the basic diet of millet, water, grits and minerals. Offer hard-boiled eggs, bread, bread soaked in fresh milk, buttered bread, peanut-buttered bread, sponge cake, greens like spinach, grass cuttings, and carrot tops, soaked and sprouted millet and pieces of orange routinely.

DRINKING WATER

Society finches will drink frequently and bathe frequently. They will bathe in their drinking water and drink from their bathing dishes. You may try to force them to do it your way. You probably will not succeed. Why bother? The water should be fresh and clean at all times, regardless.

MINERALS

Lime can come from crushed cuttlebone, crushed oyster shells, crushed lime plaster out of a very *old* house or crushed boiled or baked chicken egg shells. New homes are mostly plastered or wallboarded with gypsum plaster or gypsum wallboard (calcium sulphate), but one hundred years ago hydrated lime was used for plastering. This hydrated lime became lime carbonate over the course of time, and this mineral is the traditionally proven source of calcium you should provide to your birds. Mineral grit put up especially for cage birds surely contains this chemical compound and traces of everything else that birds are known to require.

One reason cuttlebone is so highly regarded by experienced birdkeepers is to be seen in the following figures:

Eggshell of domestic chicken, 85% calcium carbonate,1.4% magnesium carbonate.

Cuttlefish bone, 85% calcium carbonate, .5% magnesium carbonate.

The reason for repeating the word "crushed" in a previous paragraph is that some fanciers believe that a society finch cannot satisfy its need for calcium by picking at large pieces of hard mineral. This is, of course, true if you offer a large block of marble statuary limestone building block, or even a shell of a cherrystone clam. Cuttlebone by contrast is so soft you can cut it with your fingernail; your zebras will have no trouble picking particles from the edges or soft side. Notice that every piece of cuttlebone does have a hard side and a soft side, so if you hang it against a wall, expose the soft side. So, crush the stone and do whatever you think is right with the cuttlebone.

For those readers who are not familiar with chemical terms associated with calcium, a short glossary is in order:

Calcium—the essential substance, a metal most people have never seen, never will. Abbreviation is Ca. It is easily combined with oxygen, water and the carbonate and sulfate radicals.

Lime—the compound calcium oxide (CaO) is properly "burnt lime." This is the solid residue from the intense heating of limestone ($CaCO_3$). When heated, limestone breaks down to CaO and carbon dioxide gas (CO_2) and the gas passes off into the atmosphere. When calcium oxide is exposed to air that contains carbon dioxide, it combines to make limestone. Limestone is the fossil remains of mollusk shells and coral and microscopic forms which were buried for eons. It sometimes has water also bound up in it. Oyster shells, cuttlebone and egg shells are chemically very similar.

Hydrated lime is calcium oxide that was soaked in water and has taken up some water in a loose bond CaO • x H_2O. Actually calcium oxide is slightly soluble in water.

One of the staple seeds for almost all small seed-eating birds is spray millet. The birds enjoy picking the small seeds from the spray. Birdkeepers find the sprays very practical, since they can visually ascertain when the seed is eaten. When seed is poured into a tray the shells mix with the seed and it is difficult to know how much feed is left for the birds. Novices often starve their birds because they don't find empty seed cups and think their birds aren't eating very much.

Gypsum is the substance of plaster of paris and wallboard. Chemically it is calcium sulphate, hydrated ($CaSO_4 \cdot x$ H_2O). A bird probably can derive its calcium requirements from it, but the more natural source is limestone.

Sick society finches are not always easy to recognize. Obviously sick birds, like the society finch shown to the left, usually sit huddled, puffed and quiet, usually low in the cage. Weaklings in the nest (see below) are those birds which develop much more slowly than their nestmates. These weaklings usually die before they leave the nest, since the parents usually stop feeding them.

Diseases

Start with healthy birds from a reliable source. Keep them dry and out of drafts. Feed them good millet and supplement the millet with other grains, green vegetables, minerals, grit and clean water. Don't introduce sick birds or even birds that haven't been in a quarantine of some sort. Let them sleep all night every night without interruption; no noisy mice, no flashing lights. Give them sufficient room.

All right, you did all that. Now enjoy your birds; chances are good they will never have a sick day. But what if they do?

First, go over the checklist of food, water, shelter—the basics. Then evaluate the damage. Did you lose one bird simply because it flew into a window and broke its neck or is there an epidemic in your aviary? Look for signs: ruffled feathers, eyes appear small, much daytime sleeping, little eating, wet vents, running nostrils, no chirping.

You will have to be a detective, because most bird diseases are hard to diagnose positively without an autopsy. There are several courses of action after you have gone over the obvious things first. See a veterinarian and be prepared to pay for the visit. He may have to work as hard on your bird as he does on Fifi the poodle.

Second, study the diseases of birds in a specialized book. There are several. Robert (Birdman of Alcatraz) Stroud's *Diseases of Canaries* (T.F.H. Publications) is applicable to society finches. Another scholarly text used by veterinarians and advanced bird keepers is Arnall and Keymer, *Bird Diseases,* T.F.H., Neptune, N.J.

PARASITES

One excellent way to keep your birds healthy is to eliminate or at least control bird lice, ticks and mites. A bird that is run down as a result of these pests cannot combat disease when it strikes. Your contribution is usually simple and inexpensive. First, for symptoms of bird lice; watch for continuous ruffling of feathers, continuous preening, continuous restlessness. Now, let's begin with a consideration of these lice and then, later on, get into the ticks and mites.

Bird Lice

The lice that bite or chew on birds are numerous and highly specialized. Let's begin at the beginning. In the animal kingdom, the phylum Arthropoda (the largest phylum) includes invertebrates with jointed limbs. Within this phylum is the class Insecta, animals in which the body is divided into three parts, abdomen, thorax and head. The head bears a pair of antennae. The thorax has three pairs of legs and often one or two pairs of wings. The abdomen is legless and wingless. This, then, is an insect. Typical are mosquitoes and the ant.

Now, among the insects there are many orders including Diptera and Mallophaga. Diptera are the insects with one pair of wings and mouth parts designed for sucking. These are the mosquitoes and gnats. Not only are they pests, but they spread disease through the saliva they inject to make the blood flow. In the aviary you should control them with fine screening and preparations containing pyrethrum.

Mallophaga are in the order of biting or chewing lice. They are avian ectoparasites. In layman's terms they live upon and derive sustenance from or through the skin and feathers of birds.

Many of them consume only the sloughed off skin and bits of feather of birds; since they do not consume living tissue they are not, strictly speaking, parasites. Others in this order do get through to the living bird through its feathers or through its skin. Still others are accidental or incidental in the aviary—for a prime example, the book louse usually found in picture frames and the pages of old books is sometimes encountered in birds' nests. It may confuse you, but hopefully your veterinarian will recognize it. Fortunately, this species is not a parasite.

Getting back to the order Mallophaga, there are two families and a host of genera and an army of species. Species is a good word—they are highly specialized. Some limit themselves to only one or two genera of birds. Others aim for a particular part of the bird such as head and neck, and others go for the long (flight) feathers. Some are fast moving and others are sluggish.

The one thing these lice have in common is that they are killed or at least kept under control by a weekly or bi-weekly dusting or water spray containing pyrethrum.

Mites and Ticks

This is one of the less pleasant aspects of birdkeeping, but it has been mastered by others over the years. The control or management routine takes time but is not at all expensive or impossible to master. To begin with the enemy, let us first know him. Better to say, let us know them, for there are quite a few. Again, they are all in the phylum Arthropoda—with jointed legs. They are not insects but rather in the class Arachnida. Now, an arachnid might superficially look like an insect, but it isn't one. This class also includes scorpions, spiders and horseshoe crabs.

As with bird lice, mites and ticks are parasites that mostly attach to the skin and suck blood. They cause anemia, and two or three ticks can consume so much blood from a newly hatched bird as to kill it. Ticks attached near the eyes can cause blindness. The saliva that enters the bloodstream of the bird is toxic and sometimes fatally so, and the eggs of these parasites, if ingested, are also sometimes poisonous.

The various mites and ticks are so similar that you should not try to recognize species. Some are so small as to defy recognition as such without a microscope. Large or blood-swollen individuals look like the ticks that attack your dog or cat. Remove them with tweezers—a dab of alcohol on the tick should help break it loose. If your bird room is heavily infested, drastic measures are in order.

Scrub and then scald the cages with water containing 5% (by weight) of washing soda. Clean the bird room thoroughly. Get down on your knees and scrub. Get into the crevices and corners.

Dust or spray your birds weekly with a pyrethrum preparation or an insecticide compounded especially for cagebirds.

Hang an anti-pest strip in the bird room *if* you can find one that is non-toxic for birds. Or move the birds out and really fumigate the area for a few days. The best drug to kill tickets and mites in the bird room (not on the birds) is gamma benzene hexachloride. Spray the entire area, especially the corners and crevices, every ten days until you have wiped out the entire pest population.

Burn all the wooden perches and replace with new. Also, get rid of the nest boxes and any other wood or wicker goods that cannot be absolutely sterilized by chemicals, boiling water or 250° F. dry heat.

There are some feather mites that do not suck blood, but since it is not easy to tell what you really have, and you certainly don't need *any* mites, you might well go after them too. Still other microscopic mites get into the quills of feathers; they have been suspected to be the cause of French molt in budgies but this has never been proved.

Scaly leg is also a disease of mite infestation. It is treated by drowning the mites in oil or drowning and poisoning them in oil and 0.02% gamma benzene hexachloride. Since the gamma benzene hexachloride is toxic to small birds in concentrations over 0.02%, you would be better advised to use preparations containing 10% benzyl benzoate. Your petshop has proprietary medicines for the eradication of these mites.

Some mites enter the respiratory tracts of birds, and although society finches are not especially vulnerable, you should be aware that these parasites exist. Unfortunately, you won't know until there has been an expensive post-mortem examination. Fortunately, healthy birds in good environments are rarely so attacked.

Don't waste your time trying to identify lice, fleas, ticks and mites. One reliable source of information about them states that of the more than a million known species of arthropods, there are more than twenty-five hundred species of lice that are associated with birds. Additionally, there are fifteen hundred species of fleas, many of which parasitize birds. Then there are the ticks and mites (more than fifteen thousand species), of which there are hundreds found only on birds. Frequently the host-parasite relation-

Society finches breed the entire year 'round. They prefer a small nest box, basket or sieve about 4½ inches cubed. The male will fill the nest with almost anything soft and weavable. The female usually lays about five eggs over the course of about a week. The eggs take about two weeks to hatch after the start of incubation. The photo on the facing page shows the nest in the author's aviary with newborn chicks and eggs about to hatch. The photo above is a closeup of this same nest.

ships are complicated. One bird may have several lice, flea and mite species on or in its skin, feathers, nasal passages or leg scales. Some of these arthropods eat other arthropods, and some limit their activity to feces or wastes that accumulate in the nest. A cage or aviary bird wholly rid of all these pests would be unusual, to say the least. You should always aim to eliminate them, but then be satisfied if you merely succeed in controlling them.

Several governmental agencies concerned with our personal health or our environmental health have established rules and guidelines for manufacturers of insect control chemicals. These rules lead to tests that should assure that the tested insecticide is not dangerous to any but a particular organism. Unfortunately, these tests are time-consuming and expensive, so much so that many proven lice, mite and tick remedies of the past are no longer in the marketplace. Worse, there are not likely to be any substitutes for them in the foreseeable future, because the cost of proving the remedies' safety would wipe out any possible profit. The old books mention preparations that may be banned by the time you read these words. Join a fanciers' association, subscribe to a magazine, talk to your pet shop proprietor. These are the only ways you will be able to keep current with the insecticide business.

If aspirin, the safest pain killer we know, was invented in 1975, it probably never would have gotten to the pharmacists; certainly it would never have been sold as a non-prescription drug before the year 2000. The cost of testing it by present U.S. standards would be prohibitive, and drug manufacturers would find their insurance premiums unbearable. Insecticides for birds likewise.

FEATHER PLUCKING

You will not confuse natural normal molting with feather plucking. The molt is a seasonal summertime thing. The molting bird does not end up with bald spots—it just looks a bit ragged for several weeks.

Feather plucking is a vice. Some birds do it to other birds. Isolate the offender and the victim or victims will recover in a month or two. Some birds do it to themselves. Frequently the cause is overcrowding or lack of minerals, especially salt, in the diet. These are things you can correct.

Sometimes mites are the irritant, and the bird tears out its feathers as it scratches its sore spots. Your pet supply store probably handles anti-plucking sprays that can be applied to the victim. They are frequently effective, but you would be well advised to search out the cause and correct it rather than to go only after the syptoms.

If you have a pair with an aggressive male and an un-cooperative female, you may be witnessing some pre-nuptial funny business. This generally shows up as a loss of feathers on the back of the neck of the female. She will pro-bably recover completely and go on to raise a big healthy family.

SOFT MOLT

If you are inconsistent about the cage lighting and do not establish a pattern for hours of light and hours of darkness, the metabolic process of your birds will be affected adverse-ly. In plain simple language they will molt out of season. This condition is termed "soft molt." The bird in soft molt never looks quite right. Its feathers will always be ragged and its over-all appearance will look wrong to you. Even if you can't put your finger on the problem precisely, you will just know something is not quite right. When this happens to you, you are changing from a bird owner into a bird keeper. But that doesn't help your bird. What the bird needs is a careful controlled astronomical clock to turn the lights on early every day or turn them off late every night so

The society finch parents start feeding their chicks about ten hours after hatching. Nestlings have mouth markings which are visible in these excellent photographs. Wild finches have distinctive markings; that is, each species has its own markings. Unfortunately society finches are a man-made variety and their markings vary according to the plumage coloration of the particular chick when it is fully feathered.

that the cage is illuminated at *regular* intervals of about 13 hours on and 11 hours off.

If this supplement to daylight is on a simple on-off clock switch, it should be accompanied by a dim night light so the birds are never stranded in total darkness when that clock turns the bright light off.

THE HOSPITAL CAGE

Your birds are naturally vigorous and disease-resistant. It is entirely reasonable to expect that a well cared for society finch could live out its entire eight to twelve years in a cage or an aviary with no medical care. The only time you might touch it would be to clip its nails.

If you should acquire an ill bird or if an accident should befall a pet finch, your primary attack should be by way of *isolation* and *warmth*. Buy or build a hospital cage. It need not be very large. A fifteen-inch cube would suffice. It should have a low perch, a water and food supply and *controlled warmth*. Controlled warmth is a big item in the cure of most cage bird ailments, and for these little fellows 85° or 90° Fahrenheit is what they need.

A heater should be coupled with an adjustable thermostat. The ideal arrangements for this have long since been worked out and are available through pet dealers. If you feel you cannot afford the manufactured product, look at one and adapt the design. The best source of heat is electricity—25 watts will probably suffice, 50 would be more than ample. The adjustable feature of the thermostat is important, because after the bird recovers from its ailment, the temperature should be lowered to that of the normal room gradually over the course of several additional days before ending the treatment. For egg binding, colds, constipation and general malaise, you begin with warmth and then treat the specific symptom if you are able to recognize it.

MOLTING

Your healthy, normal birds will probably molt once a year, beginning in July or August and continuing for about two months. They will never be unable to fly and will appear bald or naked. A feather here, a feather there, you won't miss them, but you will notice them on the floor.

Since males and females and juveniles look pretty much alike, you should not expect any dramatic changes in color or markings during the first molt or any subsequent molt.

Don't fuss with special foods to carry the birds through the molting—if they are properly nourished they will manage to manufacture a few feathers from what they had been eating all along.

If a feather grows in twisted or broken you might want to pluck it rather than wait a year for the next molt. If you pull a feather, it will be replaced in less than a month.

NAILS

The normal length of the four nails on each foot is perhaps 1/16 or 1/8 inch longer than the part with a blood supply in it. If the nails grow corkscrewed or overly long, perching and even hopping will become difficult. Should such a long-nailed bird attempt to incubate a clutch of eggs, it will surely puncture a few.

Clip the nails with a fingernail clipper or small sharp scissors. You will be able to see the blood vessels when you look through the nails toward the light. Clip 1/16 inch beyond the end of this pink portion. If you inadvertently draw blood, and really this is unnecessary, touch the claw end with a styptic pencil or a little alum powder and the slight bleeding will immediately stop.

Many birds go through their years of life with no nail clipping, so don't do it on a routine basis, but rather on an as-needed basis.

1. This chocolate and white society finch has produced a nest of chocolate and brown chicks, but their individual markings will differ slightly. Their mouth markings are all the same. 2. A cinnamon and white society finch. 3. A chocolate and white (but mostly white) society finch. 4. Another light-colored cinnamon. Photos 2 and 3 by G. Ebben.

2

3

4

BROKEN LIMBS

Once in a great while a caged society finch will break a leg or a wing. Many bird keepers have kept hundreds of finches for decades and never had it happen, but it might.

If this is as a result of frail bones caused by a calcium deficiency you should look to minerals and vitamin D. If the problem is in the cage design the answer will be obvious.

What to do with the injured bird? You decide, but here are a few hints and guidelines. Splints consisting of a ¼-inch by 3/8-inch piece of transparent household mending tape have been used by some fanciers with success. A hospital cage with no perches, quiet isolation, warmth and rest sometimes suffices for a spontaneous mending of a broken bone. Amputation is sometimes necessary. One-legged birds will thrive for their normal lifespan, but they will not breed, since both legs are necessary for a bird to keep its balance during copulation.

Wings are even less frequently broken, and they generally mend in a hospital cage within three weeks with quiet isolation. There is not much you can do about a broken wing on a finch, but if you wish to go to the expense, you might consult your veterinarian.

PRECAUTIONS

If you are interested in adding birds from another aviary,do it only if you are absolutely sure of the health of the new birds.

If in doubt, isolate the newcomers for at least two weeks, preferably in another building, at least in another room. Don't be the carrier of disease as you go from newly introduced birds to your own valued stock.

A bird can kill itself by a broken neck or fractured skull if it flies full speed ahead into a closed window. *If* your aviary has some glass windows you may discover that frightened birds fly into them. Spray a little whitewash or paint on each window pane so that it doesn't look like all outdoors and the birds will avoid it.

Birds with broken wings should be isolated in a small cage where they cannot fly. Their wings heal quickly if the bird is kept inactive.